With sonorous cadences, with relentless honesty, and with deeply human truths, as well as deeply human humans infusing her poems, Maria Nazos has written a stunning first collection. Godspeed (like a bolt, like a bullet) *A Hymn That Meanders* into the world!

      Thomas Lux, author of *Particles: Poems, The Cradle Place, The Street of Clocks*, and *New and Selected Poems, 1975-1995*.

Maria Nazos's first book successfully depicts an 'us' whose lyric motion is equal parts devotional and destructive but never accidental—like a handbook of the ways, when coupled in couplets, we either invent versions of romance and freedom for each other or we do not. Not one of these poems will waste your time musing or poeticizing. This is grown-folk poetry, up front and adult, and there is not an ounce of surface-utterance in *A Hymn that Meanders*.

      Thomas Sayers Ellis, author of *Skin Inc: Identity Repair Poems* and *The Maverick Room*.

A HYMN THAT MEANDERS

OTHER BOOKS FROM WISING UP PRESS

WISING UP ANTHOLOGIES

Illness & Grace, Terror & Transformation

Families: The Frontline of Pluralism

Love After 70

Double Lives, Reinvention & Those We Leave Behind

View from the Bed: View from the Bedside

*Shifting Balance Sheets: Women's Stories of Naturalized
Citizenship & Cultural Attachment*

WISING UP PRESS COLLECTIVE

Only Beautiful & Other Stories
Kerry Langan
Keys to the Kingdom: Reflections on Music and the Mind
Kathleen L. Housley
Last Flight Out: Living, Loving, and Leaving
Phyllis A. Langton
The Sanctity of the Moment: Poems from Four Decades
Heather Tosteson

A HYMN THAT MEANDERS

Maria Nazos

Wising Up Press Collective
Wising Up Press
Decatur, Georgia

Wising Up Press
P.O. Box 2122
Decatur, GA 30031-2122
www.universaltable.org

Catalogue-in-Publication data is on file with the Library of Congress.
LCCN: 2011929742

Wising Up ISBN-13: 978-0-9827262-4-2

For me, a landscape does not exist in its own right, since its appearance changes at every moment; but the surrounding atmosphere brings it to life—the light and the air, which vary continually. For me, it is only the surrounding atmosphere, which gives subjects their true value.

—Claude Monet

TABLE OF CONTENTS

ARS POETICA WRITTEN DURING SLEEP DEPRIVATION

I should begin by saying, over dinner last night, over swirling wine
in which trees reflected like jade daggers, a friend asked me

whom I write about. I should begin by saying I deflected the question,
by asking her the same. To which she replied, "My lovers."

I'd forgotten about mine, and I should begin by saying some loves I've left,
and some have died. Some lovers dying since birth; dying

to find out what their lives are worth. One lover I've left: Joliet, Illinois, the
prison town. Its bars shook so hard they burst

open like a spider lily. Out skitter its children: I write for Jimmy Jameson,
lower lip permanently swollen

with cherry tobacco. Jimmy who hears voices of the divine I call poetry,
which I need to make sing. He never returned from those acid trips.

Whatever the reasons I did—certainly not common sense, or strength—I do
reverence to each day. Somewhere he's still bowing

over the pool table. His eternal clock, the click of the cue ball against the
eight. I write for Helen Storrow, who staggered

into our hormonal parties with a satin ribbon of blood seeping from her
nostril. The other kids said "slut," said "junkie."

They laid her to rest, but her body resurfaced on the cover of men's
magazines, her legs strewn with silver lamé.

I write for Korbin (who loved those country roads so much, he'd do ninety to feel his insides rise). His body, then spirit rose up from the car.

I write for Sherry Niles, who, after her fourth abortion hung herself like a robe on her bathroom door.

Of course, how dare I forget, I write for the humpbacks off the Cape, the whale-watch boat I worked on, for its rum-pummeling captains,

and for the man, also from the heart of the land, who worked with me. The one who took off, into his mother's basement.

When I asked him where he would go next, he said, "I want to live in the clouds." I didn't understand him until now, as I write this for all of us

who live on the clouds; for the wild sweet place we've put ourselves, for the sky that never parts, for the lovers who do.

And what makes you think
        we'd ever want
                to leave this place?

I
JOLIET

WILD, WILD HORSES

PAINTING OF A TRUCK

But when you look closer: a man and woman lounge in the front of his
bloodrust pickup. Her body's half-spilling out of the ajar door, bare feet

slung through the open window, as if this accident called life is gentle.
They're wrong for each other: love premature as a robin's egg waiting to
meet gravity on a dark lawn—

maybe he works with his hands: a painter. A carpenter. His hair's shucked
corn. He sinks pool balls into pockets with one fluid swoop.

She has a snap to her voice she's picked up from a city and can't put down.
He sands her sharp words until they're no longer blunt.

Should I keep describing us, after objectivity fails and sentiment takes over?
Distance doesn't work. But I'm afraid that if I love you,

my ribcage will cave in on my heart, like a miner who has spent his last
second breathing gold. A man and a woman can't go anywhere

without hard work and argument. We sat in the truck, lord knows how
long: not going anywhere, not working, not arguing, until the storm
gave up.

I've decided to leave us there. For the rain to keep freckling the windshield,
for us to stop hammering logic on this world (an effort erratic

as the heart, yet incessant as its beats). For each day to go on not caring if
we do. I've decided for us to love this strange world—

for as long as we can stand to be in it.

BACK TO JOLIET

Joliet: the Sauk, the Fox, the Kickapoo led by Black Hawk, with a crimson
flame for a mohawk, fought the floods

of settlers they called the Big Knives. Though nothing about them was
silver, except the lead mines they pillaged, pillaged in Joliet.

Joliet, taken away from her love, Romeoville, when the name was changed.
Joliet: ancestors hailing from islands of white

granite, where the sun glinted against gray-green fish loaded into baskets in
the morning market. Ancestors who left hard soil and wild

black goats. The woman with brown braids. The young man on cobblestone
streets who wanted only to touch her braid,

and did. They married, crossed the dark ocean to Joliet. The woman in
braids had a daughter who, years later,

said to her own grown daughter, *write it down*. And her daughter said, *I
wrote it*. Joliet, the slow buzz of the motorized saw. *Joliet*,

the Rock Run Forest Preserve. *Joliet*, where killers are put down. Joliet,
where steel bars burst open.

Joliet: where the daughter leaves her dark-plaited mother and returns to the
hard-soiled island with its wild black goats

and finds her own young man, a captain, eager to touch her hair. Leaves
him there and goes back to Joliet, exchanging yearning

letters intercepted for years by the dark-plaited mother. And still they marry,
daughter and sea captain, and sail the African coast,

where female forms carved out of sleek tusks are sold by natives. The stars
become a terrible magnet. She is pulled, from the ocean, pulled

back to Joliet. Joliet, she jokes, where I spent half my life trying to get out
and the rest trying to get back in. She misses the soft soil,

and so here she raises the babies, calls her mother. And does not sleep. Here
she drinks wine each night and in the bathroom cries, *Joliet*.

And here, in Joliet, her gray-plaited mother dies. In Joliet, the woman sits at
the window. Plays records that remind her of paisley,

of freedom, while the porch is studded with lightning bugs. She glares at the
captain, his temples as silvered as hers.

She calls her sister. She watches the earth tilled. Watches hot white lights of
nail salons and drug stores burst up, remembers a distant ocean fall

on Joliet's deaf ears and blind eyes. Hears Indians cry at night, rise from
misted graves to ghost this land that stole their soil, dark

as the manes they cling to. When she presses her head against the screen,
over the whine of mosquitoes, she can hear them whisper:

Joliet, Joliet, Joliet.

WILD, WILD HORSES

I remember Jim's Rack 'n Cue, in those pockets of time between sleep and awake; those times my mother let me out of the house

long enough to dart into the silver smoke clouds gilding the ceiling. The way the bottles on the dusty bar gleamed

under the fluorescent lamp, and of course, Jimmy Jameson. His flannel hung undulant, unbuttoned. Bowing like a reed over the meadow

of the pool table. His eyes black as bonfires put to ash and reignited. When Korbin had words to say, Jimmy dragged

him into the parking lot, slammed his head against his pickup truck door, took him down in a pyre of fists and torn shirts.

I remember Jimmy pulling into my impossibly long driveway. Said my life was perfect, as the light

flooding the front door was eclipsed by my mother's bathrobed form. She'd drink, smoke, and lecture, but believed in college degrees,

though not in me. Someday I'd leave the house, destined for a future she shone in my eyes like a policeman's flashlight.

Jimmy wasn't in school anymore. His parents I almost never saw, just heard when his mother's voice called

through the wafer-thin ceilings for us to keep it down. He'd reply, "It's always somethin' ain't it?" Those nights and mornings he stayed up, wild as those horses in the song. I wanted to tell him it isn't a sin to fall, but to fall from no great height.

But one day on the phone, his mother said in a flat tone that Jimmy wasn't well, that he wasn't making sense, that he was telling her the devil

lived in her eyes, that he had gone. The wild horses that sent him into this life dragged him out flailing so hard he left a dust-angel.

Back then I had a dream of six horses, tawny, dark, ginger and white, paraded onto ice by proper jockeys. Suddenly the shatter,

and the horses going down, and the jockeys falling also, and how I wanted them to be pulled out, but their hooves flailed, their teeth

pulled back to show the pink, their lean muscled necks thrashed and strained, as they slid further into the ice—

I woke, knowing I wouldn't hear from him. Until years later, from the free mental health clinic payphone.

So I have not seen him go down kicking, have not seen him descending. Instead I have imagined him rising with icicles curled into his hair.

Nights I walk the beach, swearing that if I stare long enough, wild horses will emerge from dark surf.

I want to touch those animals, but there's no saving a wild animal or man who surfaces from his own darkness

like a voice in the night, a stranger calling a stranger from a payphone.
But just because I can't reach him

doesn't mean he isn't rising from the waves on his own white horse,
riding bareback out of himself into the brief bruise of day,

as if to say, I've beaten you.

A NIGHT BACK IN JOLIET, ILLINOIS

You'd better start believing in God,
said Korbin one night.

Home for the first time in light
years, I'd smashed a girl's head into the wall

for calling him a cokehead, which was true,
but from her mouth felt like a shirt sleeve

whipping in the night breeze. Shame settled like a curtain of soot.
Joliet people didn't regret their fights.

They talked about wins or losses as if buying shoes, or falling in love.
Korbin said he needed God when he dried out

in a cabin with his last earnings, when he called
the woman at the bank. She wired him money. They loved.

At nineteen, even with no cartilage in his nose and planets
reflected in his eyes, he was blessed—

While I, dressed in armor, charged blind into a blank
pasture: a miracle I had no business being in.

INFINITE THINGS

If what I see outside myself is what I see inside myself, then why
I am back in my hometown, the only one awake,

besides two young men and a bottle of spiced rum we're about to murder,
is that the world inside me is dead.

Korbin says people like me who shy away from war like a gasoline-soaked
door are called freeloaders:

someone who mucks through life, a half-spastic fugitive survivor who never
fought. But I want to care about infinite things:

about a man in Iowa who wrapped a scarf of two-tone blue around my bare
shoulders as I awoke one morning and said,

that's your spirit color; want to care about poetry, and about the gods
of chance, but these days, even this

doesn't feel like enough. I fear that I have misplaced my passion like a pair
of earrings. You're a Ferrari

stuck in neutral, said my father. As both boys pound the table and chant
U-S-A, and I don't feel anger,

I wonder how long this coasting can go on. Then, Jimmy asks, What do you
fear? What do you really fear? And I say, America.

And he and the other boy stop thumping. America?, they ask. Suddenly, I
am not afraid to say it. So I say, America. Fuck America.

And because it gets them angry, I say it again, Fuck America. I fear nothing
except old age and death in bed and

America. None of it true, but the way I arouse these men's wounded looks,
and the drinking, and the dimensionless

dialogue that comes with it forces me to look at myself in light unflattering
as a dressing room's—

look at that self, saying it first softer, then loudly, I hate America, fuck
America. And I feel the slow heartbeat of the world stir back up,

myself, in love all over again.

A LIFE BEYOND THAT PLACE

WATCHING BERGMAN FILMS WITH MY MOTHER

And now the man plays a trick on the woman's psyche. He hides her keys
again and again, until she falls

victim to first her own intellect, then his. Perhaps a woman can be too
smart. And this makes her vulnerable.

Makes me think of my mother. She's sitting on a plaid couch, in a seashell-
pink bathrobe, on her third gin: a misty cloud

in the tumbler that dissipates to show no sky. Now she's put the tiny orange
pyre of a cigarette in her mouth.

Thirty years she's been trying to quit, thirty years, and still all show,
no go. Once she had what we all want: degrees, hopes

higher than the planets and just as aligned. A Greek isle she landed on,
unexpectedly as the monarch that rubs its wings,

not knowing it will begin a monsoon several lines of latitude away. She
meets a young sea captain with eyes bright as wild fruit, and hair

like the vines of wild fruit also. He doesn't promise her the world, but the
circumference. And so they sail. And what happened from there:

her feeling stuck on the ship with nothing but constellations whose names
she could never memorize. Trying to take up knitting,

then crocheting. Testing out her shaky Greek like a new bike, taping her
voice and sending the cassettes

to her mother-in-law. Her husband asking her, what's wrong in a way that
demands anything but an answer

that wasn't glittering with the ions of the ocean. When the babies came, she
said it was the first time she'd fallen in love. My mother,

like Bergman, prisoner of a man's brain, shackled to the sink, cold water
piping her wrists, words pumping

through her like hormones, *this is what you want*. My mother, like Bergman,
developed Stockholm syndrome with her body,

her male captor. And I'd run from our high-tax-bracketed home down
Black Road to Jimmy's house. His stepfather built the place

so the doors hung the wrong way. His mother gave us frothy rum-spiked
drinks. Laughed with her whole body.

I wonder if the things a woman thinks she wants (the sleek black cat of a
car, the landscapers, the degrees white as the ivory

tower they fell from, the babies) aren't enough. When the wedding dress
flags surrender, has a man lost your car keys, taken you out to sea?

I have the answer when a whale throws its thirty-ton body from the ocean
like a question mark, a behavior scientists can't explain.

I realize a woman's reasons for hurting will never surface, will never be
known. Her heavy sadness doesn't rise, just flashes

across her face like silver fish in black waters. I'm certain then that there's
something bigger.

And all I have before me, even her story, this movie, is pure nature.

A QUESTION ABOUT CAUSE AND EFFECT

If he weren't born to a mother who smoked Marlboro Lights, if he weren't
stuck in the spit-sized, die-while-you're-dark-haired-

on-a-country-road town but in a city, if he'd been born at the tip of Cape
Cod, to a painter or professor, if it was in a university dorm

he was able to bend his head to another man's groin—would there have
been an inward struggle? Would the rumors have spread like oil,

the scorn burn behind the local women's eyes? Without the word faggot
slamming like hammers on anvils, would he have found

the words, *my choice, freedom, experiment?* Or would he still have come at
his past lover. Grabbed his shirt,

said, *You're the faggot.* Would he have raised his eyes to the mirror and
embraced him as beautiful, or a passing experiment?

Would he have accepted a man's love isn't always poured into the rigid
mold of a woman's body, that it can take the shape of a man?

Would he have peeled off sticky sexual labels to reveal his heart, held a girl
(whose only concern was his arms do the same)

instead of chanting in the mirror, *I'm sick, I'm sick, I'm sick,* until he
checked into a mental health clinic? Or does this chalk outline

of a hate crime spread across America? If he'd had proper health care, would
he have lived, or at least opened a window

so the warm breeze swept back the curtains, like a woman's hair off her shoulders? If he'd not been at the shelter,

would he have turned his hate-compass away from his absent mother, his stepfather who pulled a gun on him;

would he have learned anger as communication? If he'd grown up outside of a school that was mostly dark

faces locked in the heartland that didn't open except to swallow them whole would the word "nigger" have burnt its cross on his mind?

If he had not been born to a mother who didn't lay nightly beneath her boyfriend's quick fist and temper,

and if the girl he loved hadn't run away to the East Coast, to a place of different politics, because, she too could never quite place the words,

just pose the question before the mirror, in the arms of different lovers and cities that half-embraced her:

If they'd met in another life, less beautiful, less cruel, could this have been love?

MY MOTHER'S NIPPLES

—after Robert Haas

I remember them: freakishly large, pink nubbins and the way she would swathe a towel around her head and step naked from the shower—

Concave stomach, lower abdominal slope, the wiry black grove of pubic growth. I remember my mother's nipples—not when it mattered, not when I bit the breast that fed me—but years later.

*

An ancient Greek myth my mother read to me as a child: Hercules was being breastfed by Hera, but unbeknownst to her, he was the product of one

of her philandering husband's many affairs—she'd have been wild had she known—but nonetheless, decided to breastfeed baby Hercules; not recognizing him

as the same child who crushed two white vipers she'd sent out to kill him upon his birth. And the way my mother looked up at this point in the story,

"Now don't get the idea that Hera likes baby Hercules," she said. "She doesn't. She's just breastfeeding him." Back to the story: Hercules bit down

on Hera's nipple, sending her spray exploding across the sky, where it stayed. This was how the Milky Way came to be.

*

Those years we lived in Greece, the house was marble encased by a white balcony, and it was white, all white, in fact, with gargantuan columns, and the yard was dirt with a single palm in the middle, and kumquat trees and figs bursting with mealy fecundity; the same bruised, purple inside as a nipple. And the yard smelled of a hundred, bleating, breeding tomcats. My mother was wild with loathing for the cats. She would stand outside, at the top of the marble stairs that glinted in the sun, and would hiss and stomp until the cats would scatter like terrified krill under rocks. Refused to drive or walk outside of the house, because she claimed she once saw a naked man in the bushes on the way to the kiosk to buy cigarettes. She was always calling her aging mother in Illinois and crying that she wanted to leave this place. Nights, she and my father would go to wild Carnival parties: I saw the photos of my aunt dressed as a hula dancer with bare shoulders and a pair of plastic breasts, topped with hard nipples. She was sitting with my mother, who told me that at the last minute she put on a white puffy wig she'd brought along, and at the party borrowed my aunt's mascara to paint large, black spots on her face right before a woman at the party got on a glass table to dance and fell over. "They were beauty marks," she explained.

*

The first woman's nipples I ever felt, except my own: Sherry Niles's. Eight years ago in Southern Illinois, where we moved after my mother's mother fell ill. I asked Sherry what she'd like me to do. She refused to answer. I recall the way she felt, the way they felt: like two hard little knots, two stubborn buds that refused to break through to the surface, that withheld their secret and kept you guessing at the beauty they might contain.

*

In 1967, my mother left the University of Chicago. Whether she dropped out or was kicked out is unknown. All I have managed to discover of my mother's early adulthood comes from the beautifully slurred words of drunk relatives at family parties. "She went to Greenwich Village with three blacks," said my grandmother. "Three Black Panthers, I remember. She was calling me every hour to check in. God knows what would have happened, had I found out then! She was in love with one of them, one of the blacks."

My grandmother leaned in. Her glasses magnified her eyes until they looked as big as twin dinner plates, and under the lenses, just as glossy. "Shhhhh... never repeat this..."

*

When we moved to the US, which, all this time, my mother so adamantly said she wanted to do, and left my father in Greece to captain boats, my mother would often sit in our new house in Joliet, Illinois, and drink tumblers of gin in the plaid living room and the big house we bought that she said she'd always wanted seemed to loom even larger around her, in her seashell-pink bathrobe on the couch. Often the bathrobe drooped, revealing her one brown nipple. Her breasts hung lower than I remembered, her mascara smudged. around her eyes, her hair wet and dark as a seal's. She would drink until her face flushed, excited and feverish. Sometimes she would tell me it was entirely my fault, the fact that she was self-destructing, because I never helped clean up the house, and the house was dirty, dirty. Then she would get some Clorox, dump it in a bucket, and start cleaning the floor. Every night, I felt something inside of me break. Usually I would yell back. I would curse until words flew out of my mouth like black moths. Mostly, though, she would sit on the couch and drink.

*

The first man who ever saw my nipples was Jimmy Jameson. Eleventh grade. On the floor of a friend's empty apartment in Joliet, Illinois. I told Helen , a friend more experienced than I. "Isn't it great?" she said, and shook my hand. She would later drop out of school, go on to become addicted to heroin, then suddenly clean up and win a TV modeling show. She went on to pose for *Playboy*, and years later, I see her: splayed naked on a cream-colored floor, her legs longer and more tragically beautiful than a Russian novel, with crossed feet in silver high heels resting against a gilded couch. The first woman to hear about my first nipple-play: more intimate than when Jimmy first saw them.

*

Years later, I ran off to Cape Cod, and worked at a dessert café. The owner's wife made chocolates: amazing replicas of bodily appendages. My gay friend who worked with me took one look at a breast lollypop: bright white with a nipple in the center like a maraschino cherry. The color was a bright fuchsia like the stamen of a flower.

"Nipples are not that color," he said.

"Yes they are. They can be, I mean. I promise." I said. "They can be different colors according to, you know, arousal."

"Not that color, though."

Behind the barista station, I pulled down the front of my blouse to expose my left breast. "See?" I said. "mine are a coffee-color. All different colors."

He almost fainted. "I see," he finally said.

*

I used to watch my mother put on makeup before going to a party in Greece. She would make her face pale with foundation. ("In my day it was considered elegant to be pale," she said.) Then, she would dot her face with burnt sienna lipstick and rub it in. Then, my favorite part, the way she held her hand steady, and drew a freehand, blue-black line across her eyelid. She had to be the most beautiful woman in the world.

*

One night, I was lying in bed and it was one of those nights, I had to have been one of the only people left awake in the world, and my mother came into my room. She was usually drunk at this time, but for once, she was sober. She came over to the edge of my bed. "Mind if I sit here?" And perched at the edge of it for a minute. Her frame was small in her pink robe, but she sat very tall, very straight. For once she didn't sway as if blown by some imaginary breeze. She did not smell liquory, but instead fresh, out of the shower, like White Rain Shampoo, a hint of sweat. She was very quiet and sat for very long. The night, it seemed, sat quiet and very long also. The moon washed her features in its pale glow. For some reason, this is all I return to; she seemed very lonely, but very strong. It is a scene that never begins and never ends. Somewhere in time, the mother is sitting at the edge of her daughter's bed, and the transition is not a transition, but a moment in which the ego drops away and a person reveals himself or herself beyond the struggle with diction. This is all I have. All I return to.

HYMN TO THE MIDWEST THAT MEANDERS

You can take the girl out of white-trash Joliet, but you can't take the white-trash Joliet out of the girl, no matter how many poems she may write.

—*an ex-love from Dubuque, IA*

It's true: I can't remove myself from Middle America. From visions of people who keep surfacing in my poems: from Jimmy,

whose large hands were poems, Jimmy, whose cheekbones I see in each derelict, a constant x in this world's equation of sanity—

Jimmy with his once impish brown eyes staring blank-eyed out the barred window into the one white strip of light from the courtyard below.

I say the one prayer left to me. For those trapped in the middle-part of America, where kindness is yanked tightly

across the land, like a bed sheet I could bounce a nickel against. For the niece, whose life stretched before her and whispered

of a life beyond that place. For the illness I've refused to write because it doesn't put her in an accurate light: call it

a woman's hunger strike against the world. For the mother, wilted in a suburb; she looks for her sea captain

husband through an empty bottle's bottom. For the girl who sat in class writing stanzas in her geometry notes,

who everyone said was too strange for this world. For the red striated muscles of Colorado. For the hurricane that strikes twice. For the girl who knows she is not too strange to know the raped baby in Uganda whose eyes already stare out

at a warped and vacant world. World, I say, as if this world stops when the land begins to rise and the oceans also and the hills

spring up, and the rainforests sing with undiscovered cures, and the humpbacks breech from the sea, and the gannets glide down to meet their open mouths.

II
PROVINCETOWN

IS THIS THE MOST BEAUTIFUL MOMENT
IN YOUR LIFE?

THANKSGIVING HOTSPOT

—Provincetown, MA, 2007

"We come to Cape Cod to heal or die," says Captain Dan Tubb. Half-
drunk with a beard and eyes like a pre-storm sea,

a bottle of Bermuda rum tucked under his arm. He's captain of the whale-
watch boat. He agitates white-sided dolphins by steering

the ship to churn the wake, spots a humpback blowhole, then closes into
fifty of their spouts. Propped against my doorframe

in a fedora, he says, "Call me Esta-tubb," slurring his words like scallops,
cool and slimy in his mouth.

After Louise left bruises over his eyes like kiss imprints at Lugg's Place, he
donned a pair of dark glasses and trailed here. The humpbacks

have migrated to the Caribbean. But nobody knows where Minke whales
go. Now, Dan strums a few dark chords until he breaks

into "Hot Spot," a song about a man who comes to the Cape to find what
life is about but winds up at a bar, which seems

very sad this evening, yet all of us are singing. The first mate, Murray was
left as a baby on a doorstep. Tonight, he's trying not

to remember his woman, mad, beautiful Sally, who descended the stairs,
swirling an iron by its cord. Tonight, I am trying too; trying to not

remember my hometown in Illinois, known only for its prison. The people, despite their racism and sexism are good.

But this doesn't change the intensity with which I hate that place. I can't help but feel as though I've found the hotspot. Shucked like an oyster.

No pearl. Dan Tubb takes our fire extinguisher, sprays the living room cold, the hot spot smothered in foggy blast—

I won't need ever to look beyond this.

AFTER THE WHALE WATCH

On the captain's skiff, I press my cheek flat against the boat as if listening to
a heartbeat nobody else can hear,

as if in the throes of a slow dance. Murray, the first mate, laughs from the
bow. "Women are pretty when they aren't crazy."

It's too late in the day to argue gender politics after hours of watching
whale spouts, and landlocked, slack-jawed tourists

who hail from the heart of the land: a place I am trying to forget—along
with you. A fisherman throws a live lobster onto our skiff.

Murray tugs the antennae until they cross and thrash like twin lighthouse
beams; a man of the land and a man of the ocean

locked in a battle of elements. And the lobster is shamed and still not taking
it—unfurling its claws and lashing at anything it can, even me.

With no choice but to confront this small fear that hates me, this scorpion
of the ocean still snapping

its claws, I've backed to the stern of the boat. Murray says, "that there's a
Portuguese watchdog."

I need to be backed to the end of the boat as if walking a gangplank. I need
a bell-ringer of a watchdog to watch me

in this moment so different from my landlocked life, need something to erase your memory, to push me to the end of the world as if dancing

on the edge of a sharp knife. (Your beauty also is a very sharp knife.) Need a lobster, a knife, anything

fierce enough to distract, to remind me in the next breath that you are everywhere, to remind me

to stay here, on the world's edge instead of the white-hot center.

AMERICAN ROMANCE

I'm in the galley, watching rows of tourists scream at the rainbows streaking
from the blowholes. Can't pretend I don't hail

from the same place. Neither can you. Although you're not choked with
corn. And you're dark as a humpback's shadow. And you're playing

bass next to Captain Dan, who steers barefoot at the wheel. You're trying
desperately as I to escape the heart

of a land that never let us in. You left me remembering: us on the flying
bridge with granules of salt stuck in our eyebrows,

watching humpbacks float up to the boat. How I hate this country so much
bigger than us—that, like us, doesn't have the sense

not to fight. Unlike the shy whales, hollow zeppelins of air: they're peaceful.
They have no choice but to put up with us, shrieking

masses. Maybe the whales want to overtake this boat. Maybe they see us for
the frauds we are: we seemed to love each other,

seemed not to see seagulls eat one another, not to smell the greasy linguica.
Back then I tried to make the scene pretty.

I didn't see your face for what was behind it, the whales for what was inside
them, these tourists for their excitement

that was the same as mine, or Middle America for the sweet naiveté it carries like a fat child-faith.

I didn't see what I see now: a place better than love alone can make.

THE FIRST PERSON

I've been the man who has fucked four times a day, you say, struggling to
get your pants back on like a better-fitting skin.

And I've been that woman, I want to say. Though that woman seems
as far away as I was from the you, until I'm sure it's possible to escape

not through your skin, but by shifting focus from the first person to third,
like a camera lens, or the pupil of an eye

exposed to dark, then light, then dark—Rilke said metaphysical. I call it
plain goddamned human.

This woman and the man—because perspective has changed—are walking
the blond dunes. She's afraid to graze his hand.

They've found a tiny puddle. Upon further examining, the puddle is filled
with fish the color of the sand dunes and why,

she's thinking, are those flecks of rainbows in the water? Why do we try to
slip out of our bodies with this drunkenness, sobriety, happiness,

melancholy, with this escape to the world's edge? Why this emphasis on
time when it doesn't exist?

By now, the water expands. The woman's no longer sitting before the
puddle, but in it. The pool of water

grows larger and more of the strange muted fish shoot into the pool as if
spat from an invisible ocean. The fish

dart under the glittering flecks of sand when they see the man and woman's shadows. The woman realizes

the pool that she's sitting in actually is the ocean expelling itself into the dunes. The pools growing deeper and wider.

Pretty soon, there will be water everywhere, which makes sense, because people are water, aren't they? Which is why I can slip

back into the first person pronoun, back into my body, back to you and me. So the trickle of water grows louder but I'm still

afraid to touch you. Afraid of the anger, the dead crabs, the people we once were as seen through the third person lens. People

who now are not us, less so even than the ones we're about to become. I'm still afraid of the ocean that separates us. I want to escape

from the water. Return to that pure place where I feel like the first person on earth with a prayer.

So I curl into a fetal coil until a shining cord seems to hang from my belly into the sand; a connection that I've always felt,

just never seen in the right light.

LOVE POEM TO A TREE

After you and I stayed too late at a party between parties, I said I was
through with the fighting, for there are too many fights

in this world. Say it to the tree, you said. The tree's shadow quivered in the
window like an orgasm

in the dark, and your hair was wild as an undersea flower, and I said to the
tree, "I want to love you," and you asked me

to say it again, and so I said, "I want to love you," which I thought the
same as telling you, because everything is connected.

But then you went back to Iowa. And I felt the empty hiss between my
shoulders. How difficult to speak

to a world whose beauty reflected blank loss: from the breakwaters, to the
sand dunes, to every face. All the while wanting everything

to tell me you'd be back from the endless cornfields. But no
thing replied. The world seemed a hollow

canyon without echo I'd call into for you, only you. Until without warning
you're present again in everything. Even that tree: and now I can speak—

I hate this earth for burying you standing up. I demand to know why.
But the glittering dunes refuse to answer.

The deserted lobster pots on the docks refuse to answer, and the fishermen
(whose skin, like old boxing gloves, I've searched, hoping

to find yours underneath) refuse to answer. I keep saying, "I want
to love you." But words are impossible to say

to the one who was never here. Even so I keep saying, "I want to love you."
Until I come to love this strange world.

With or without you in it.

MINK ROOFTOP

We ended up on a seaside rooftop, sipping champagne from flutes with two women who had just gotten married—

one in a pear-colored tuxedo and closely cropped hair, the other in a brown lace dress with canary pin curls—attended by two old queens

in black fedoras. When the bride brought out a mink the same color as the swirls in a cherry-wood floor, you pointed at me, your hair

wild beneath your cowboy hat and just as dark as your eyes, wide with the pot we'd smoked. You wanted me

to get into the mink naked; it seemed as natural as exhaling. Maybe you thought I wouldn't do it—all I have are pictures that prove it.

Slaughters of mauve, pink, and yellow flowers garnish the rooftop; the fog is the color of a widows' gray streak. I hold a rose

with dark-edged petals between my teeth and a glass of champagne. You kept photographing as I opened the coat partway,

like a shy curtain. I'm laughing with my head thrown back so far my fillings show. Now you've gone. Now this harbor town has snapped up

like a suitcase, and the fishermen are stranded in bars where they misplace memory like lost coins. Now I'm stuck in this room telling myself we were more than two broken sticks rubbing together. It was a moment, said a friend.

That's all. Like flowers pressed in a book. As I sit in this room with the rain coming down on all sides, a moment like that in the picture,

when the question was more important than the answer, I remember the one you asked that day, amid the fog and glittering salt:

"Is this the most beautiful moment of your life?"

SMASHING TOILETS

I'm walking home from work, trying not to allow the hurt I've packed to spill into the street like belongings from an unlatched suitcase.

Not the customer who snapped like an alligator with a bug on its nose. Nor the co-worker who said, so you're like me,

single with no life? Or how I told her: In order to empower another person, you have to empower yourself.

I feel helpless as a fish in a basket, and I'm trying to figure out where this country got off saying women can't be angry, and when

I got off saying I couldn't be angry. Just as I'm trying to decipher when the perfect moment falls to tell someone how full

of shit I think they are, I see Jim Breyers, the man who hoards so much miscellaneous junk. His house vomits onto the seashore,

then the neighboring parking lot. The town is after him to clean up: books about the physics of wind, old air conditioners, banisters—

I'm smashing toilets, he says. His driveway is, as always, a mosaic of crushed vases, pots, saucers, as if domesticity has flown into a quiet rage.

He gives me a pair of goggles to protect myself, and a hammer. I bring it down and feel the inertia, feel the fragments of the day's dialogue shatter in ceramic confetti. Someone must have really hurt you, my co-worker said to me.

And I bring the hammer down. I refuse to remember you. Men are like toilets, either occupied or full of shit goes an old saying.

I feel the anger I thought was finished. I smash another toilet. The good folks in the grocery store parking lot

pretend to look away. I let them know I am not the benign woman who fetches their coffee.

I am living to shatter and smash, to pave my patch of this gorgeous road.

THE UBIQUITOUS YOU

THE UBIQUITOUS YOU

Most of the time, the 'you' in a poem,
otherwise known as the 'ubiquitous you,'
is the addressee who signifies a lover.
—Thomas Lux

When I try to explain love to a new lover, I find no disguises this time, and
instead something catches

in my throat. All I can return to is how love isn't an emotional sparkplug
jammed into my heart, not the parentheses of arms, not

the shadows interlocked and undulant as bedclothes in song, but instead
when a woman is closing the bar on her first night.

The place is shadowed as an insomniac's eye. And all of the patrons have left
their debris: swizzle sticks, crumpled dollar bills,

drained martini glasses like the eye of a recovered addict staring out at a
blank desert. And the woman is rubbing her temples as she tries

to add up the register tape and all the sums keep coming up wrong. She
keeps trying to add and trying to add, and trying to separate

the money of the night into the designated categories: food tax, drinks, the
total, the tips payout, and feels a moth

in the light bulb of her heart. She can't do numbers. Only words, and
tonight, there are none that can save her.

And the man sitting at the bar has a shy white grin, a frayed tawny cowboy
hat. He leans over,

takes the calculator. Adds up the nighttime tallies, then shows her a trick to ensure the amount's accurate.

Then he slips the hat off his head, and puts it on hers. Now, as I try to explain how until I had a moment like that, I only

knew what love is like, then return to the scene of us that I've tried so hard to step outside of and examine critically, even as I say it,

I realize the only way in this world to love is to acknowledge simply that you were there, that I missed you,

that you just skimmed my face. Love doesn't need to be examined. But still, I return. Even when trying to talk

to another lover, to myself, to a friend, still I talk to you. I've acquired a new concept: when broken down, the heart

like any other muscle develops a new strength. Beyond that, I've learned to listen to that persistent, raw place that won't let me

turn away, that place hasn't finished listening, that place hasn't left that bar that day. Even though we ourselves, have long left.

He's still showing her what is so simple; I can't believe she doesn't see it—

HOW LONG YOU MUST BE IN THE DARK

You're a woman who's trying to forget a captain, asleep in the other room.
Not because you resent his scent you don't care to kiss

away, but because you're trying to be present for once, and need,
for some reason, to rise from the bed, to stagger to the dark

balcony with a blanket swathing your bare shoulders, to watch the ocean,
too dark for humpbacks to roil in.

The unruly strip of sea is like discarded fabric. The northeast winds churn
the way your captain does while steering the whale-watching boat.

He makes the tourists hang on for a life they never knew was so dear, a life
that you live, you—an escapee from the golden rows of corn.

From the terrace, at this dark height, the ocean and sky could be mistaken
for each other. You remember how you swore

to give up sex, then, recall something a friend said: Each time you move
eight steps forward, you take seven back, because living is a dance,

a cha-cha. So while you swore, no more lovers, in the other room lies one
who staggers off the whale watch boat barefoot

into Lugg's Place to play the blues. The crowd floods up to the stage like fish
caught in a tidal wave. How impossible not to slip

into love, when for once, you love the place you're in, when you've tried to
stave emotion back, like a torch before a gold-eyed,

unknowable beast that takes you in its jaws. And what a gorgeous mess he
is, sleeping, covers twisted at his feet.

Now, as waves match your heartbeat, you wonder if the fact you want back
in that room to rest against him is worth examining, anymore

than to ponder why you place yourself here, in the dark. You ask how long
must you be in the dark. The answer—until you learn

to see in it—finally makes sense. Just being here makes sense—waiting for
the tide and sun to wash the other room pale as bleached bone,

to wash you too into a moment you did nothing to deserve.

ADVICE TO DAN'S NEW GIRLFRIEND FROM THE GHOSTS OF LOVERS PAST

1.
Let's get this straight—if his heart were any further on his sleeve, it would be a wrist watch. He does tell time with it.

2.
Thing is, he isn't great at articulating things. I don't mean in that way that women stereotype men—words fail him, not he them. He believes

you cannot say *this sunset is beautiful*, believes that one phrase
can never encapsulate the rust and indigo streaks.

He believes that the yellow of the flowers poised on the sill is not a symbol for friendship. Those bursts of petals are what they are. You have no choice but to breathe them in and in—

3.
You need to train him to lie resourcefully. He cannot, repeat, cannot tell you that you've gained weight. If he ever does, stare into his eyes as if you can see his unborn children. He'll get the message.

4.
Ask him about those years playing with the Rock Bottom Band, about the fedoras and vests he wore, (and still sometimes wears), ask him about his former loves, ask him about his lover-of-three-women-

in-a-day past. Ask him about the infidelities, the monogamy, his ex-wife, Louise, who is still convinced the grass is aglow with uranium beams.

Make him dance on the frying pan. He doesn't think he loves your interrogation. Rest assured; he *does*.

5.
He'll never love you as much as he loves me.

Then again, he's a die-hard romantic who resurrects,
so one day he *might* love you as much as he loves me.

6.
Okay, let me be real with you for a second. If I'm going to lend you any
sound advice, if I'm going to impart any words that are resonant, or
applicable, words that you can wield, here they are:

you've got to be more stable than me. Hopefully you'll not feel monogamy
is a defunct institution and that you have to run from him

even though your blood whispers his name. Listen: this man with salt grit
stubble stumbles barefoot onto the whale-watch boat he captains

from the rowboat docked beside it. He used to stay on that cramped boat
whenever his ex-wife kicked him out—

She is short in height and temper. She has a soft frizz of blonde hair pinned
up like a tragically beautiful ballerina, wears iridescent skirts that catch
around her sandaled ankles, and smokes Pall Malls.

The boutique she works at is called Dulcinea, right on the main drag. I'm
telling you this so you can cross over to the other side of the street when you
see her.

She's ninety days sober, I hear, and that's a pretty crucial period. I'd stay
away from her if I were you.

7.
Okay, let me be really honest: when you've drunk too much, (because you drink only in excess), when your voice breaks (and it will),

do me a favor, and punch the couch instead of him.
You'll feel better in the long haul holding off.

8.
You're angry because you love him, because when you yell at him
he shuts down like a computer with a bad chip.

9.
The blue glass bottles under the lamp need to stay there. Those bottles are called blue solar water. He drinks from them while intoning the mantra, *I love you. I'm sorry.*

Please forgive me. Thank you. These words come from a book he's reading about delving into the place of zero limits in your heart. Read that book, I urge you; it's stunning. By the time you're finished, you'll understand the blue bottles.

10.
He won't always be perfect. When gravity kicks in and he descends lightly off the wagon, don't be too worried. He'll get back on soon.

11.
Admire him. Admire him to the point of envy.

12.
Tell that bartender to stay the hell away from him. She's the one with reddish-cropped hair, who works at Lugg's Place.

13.
He'll always forgive you, to the point of his detriment. Learn how to maintain your own humility, self-blame, and ability to be wrong.

14.
Love him, I urge you, or else I'm coming back to haunt you.

15.
He's always been pretty virile, but with you, he might need some Cialis. You can buy the prescription online.

16.
Don't do that! Don't do what I just did, don't ever cop out, using humor to deflect. *I love you. I'm sorry. Please forgive me. Thank you.*

Sing those words, sing them again and again. When you go on a whale watch, bend over the stern, it's the best place to watch the humpbacks.

While he's captaining, he likes to watch you lean over. He's wondering what the ocean smells like to you.

THE YELLOW JEEP

I keep telling you about synchronicity: The Yellow Jeep syndrome, when you suddenly see yellow Jeeps everywhere.

At the gas station, your ex-wife's gold Jeep blinks palely behind us. Her diamond nose stud glints in the daylight,

her hair pinned up in a messy bun to show her face. Even now, she retains her beauty. You both drank like lunatics and passed blame back

and forth to keep your love going, like a candle at a party where the bonfire has been ashed out. We can never know what we want.

When my last lover, at a wedding reception, told me to put on the bride's mink coat naked, I felt I had ordered him from the Universe's Catalogue.

Until he left, with a piece of me tucked under each arm, we shone together, as two people in love do. As you did

at Lugg's Place with your ex-wife, who still shines in her gold Jeep. My last love and I shone deeply enough into each other

to reflect our darkest parts. This can be mistaken for love. How long I've felt this way, I don't know. I only know that in this moment,

the Yellow Jeep is not yellow. And you, a man forty years my senior, are not the one I projected trudging up the beach those nights, thinking I wasn't looking for anyone. We don't know what's good for us, don't know where to look

for a yellow Jeep. We don't know if the sunset moves us, or the earth sunning a different side of itself, or a lover's touch, or the drawing

in of our breath (because somewhere inside, something in us knows when we let it out, we'll fall from a great height). No, we don't know why

we get who we didn't know we could love.

THE BUDDHIST EXPERIENCES A MOMENT OF RELUCTANCE

You, the man I love, believe when adoring someone we should speak only of the positive. For example, the Buddhist dangling

off a cliff, like a line of shark chum who looks down at the dorsal fins blinking palely in the afternoon sun, then up

at the vine he is clinging to, the one extension of his pathetic life, should say, " My, but aren't the grapes beautiful."

Just as I'm about to agree, I remember another friend who says he doesn't know a single man

who isn't romantic. Women want to be, but aren't really, not over a period of time—it's true.

Now, as I'm trying to write, the baby in the apartment below starts up like a howler monkey. I wonder if some of us aren't destined

to enter this world unhappy. Even you have said, That kid cries a lot—even for a baby. What do Buddhists know anyway?

Desire, they say, is the flower of hell, but that same force erected pyramids. Desire, that space between dark and light,

that sunlit corner in the clinic for the patient to wander into—Do you mean to say that you prefer the dark?

The baby's father wants to tear his architectural work to ribbons, and he wants to do the same with that screaming child.

I tell you this. You say, impossible. A parent never resents his child. But I picture the man downstairs, how he clings

to the one vine of his sanity, not daring to glance down at the sharks below gliding serenely,

like lazy bullets; how he fixes his eyes on the soft purple grapes like a sunset, like me never daring to look down, look back.

TO LOVE, AT YOUR CONVENIENCE

A friend once told me, as we lay in a bed together in the female dark, that at
the height of ecstasy, she wanted to rip

her lover's spine from his back. Someone did something to your femininity,
I said, as she stroked my hair and we waited

in the black room, like twin flames that will never merge. When she met her
husband she told him of this urge.

He seemed to understand. Which is why I turn to you, reader, lover,
listener, and admit this: When you said you'd leave me

to sail to the breezy warmth of Havana, I wanted your spine to dissolve like
a pillar of salt in the rain—

I wanted you not to look so much like my father, who always seemed so
adrift. Who left my mother, land-locked.

How easy to love at your convenience. You told me your ex-wife took an axe
to your boat. At the time I laughed.

Said, *Women don't act that way unless you've really hurt them.* Now, I wonder
if the reason was you wanted to leave. I wonder

if you had her father's eyes, if she meant to keep you, even if keeping you
meant destroying what you love. I wonder if her hammer blows

beat the ocean, if when she threw her leg across yours before bed, she was
too tired to tear you both apart?

III
CUBA

MY VERSION OF FREEDOM

They say love is when you look at someone you want to eat and won't eat
them. Two days ago, on the roof across from us, a man cupped a pigeon

and called down to a woman in white, "Would you like to buy one?"
She nodded, would soon draw a knife around the soft circumference

of the bird's neck to cure her mother's cough. That night, a rum-weary
young man pressed his wrists together to show he felt shackled to Castro.

Yesterday, a hurricane gusted through Havana, sent chickens swirling into
the air along with the sugar cane field's ghostly smoke flares

to call for help. Today the man stands on the roof, alone. A white pigeon
bursts out of his hands. Why he allows it to escape, I don't know.

Anymore than I know why it isn't a dove or if it's the woman in white
transformed and needing to be seen off—

This is my version of freedom: where one person's paradise is another one's
prison. You've brought me here, paid my way into the country.

One day, we huddled under a steel awning while the rain banged its brains
out. You said to the man beside us, "It's rough out today."

"What is rough for you? You're rich!" he replied. As if I'm free
to overlook lives that so closely touch our own: the woman in our casa,

her husband soft-eyed, rough-palmed, who wouldn't ever hurt her
but for his love of rum. He drinks in the kitchen each day.

The woman builds a white wall around herself to keep unwanted grief out.
Her husband slowly chips away at her with every drink,

until the wall collapses to chalked rubble and a white bird escapes.
Someday the woman will be strong enough

to return to her body, to rebuild herself, to leave this ruin of a marriage.
But because I am never happy, I still see her life without the wings.

I hail from a town with steel bars. I need to learn a language other than
oppression.

COCKFIGHT

Four in the morning, the rooster keeps shrieking its useless wakeup call.
Even here in Havana, a world of digital alarm clocks, where rumba

streams out gaping car doors, he is outdated. Yet the useless optimist keeps
rising. Or maybe he's a romantic,

singing from his red-feathered gut, singing the sweetness that can stop a
heart. Or maybe I'm a romantic to think

a rooster *has* a heart. The russet feathers erupt like pieces of a forgotten sun
against the dark

of male shoulders. Wild topaz eyes, flecked brown, now pecked black. The
men place bets. The roosters, now vicious,

squeal, squawk and beat wings. Who is less mighty: those who obey
evolution, or those who transcend? Machismo is buried

inside these men's bones like a fossil. I don't understand them anymore
than the boys at my hometown bar. Boys who escaped the military

draft's cold hands, thank god, but don't have the sense to move to a city, to
see their swift kicks to each other's ribs,

their heads slammed against the windshield are useless as a rubber crutch.
I'd watch those fights

with the same feigned interest that I reserve for any outdoor sport. They'd
glide around each other

like playful animals, in the gutters of discarded pizza plates after the bars closed. The man I love

has large hands that could crush me, but would never. He dodged the draft that would have sent him straight

to the rice paddies. He lied like oil to the doctor at his pre-enlistment check-up, said *I caught jungle rot while in the Amazon,*

his medical records shaking against his knee. The doctor stamped his physical REJECTED FOR MILITARY SERVICE.

Like a rooster who rises each day to crow, my man kept singing, *I will not pick up a brick, shovel, or gun for a country I'm not proud of.*

My man let others call him what they would: *longhairs, faggot, lazy, commie.* He let the other men circle and cross each other out.

Then moved to a harbor town. Drank Bermuda rum at noon in a bar with fishermen. Made music at night, his hand curled around a guitar

like a woman's waist. I will never be brave enough to rise and sing knowing others won't listen. Can only write this hoping

someone will read it and remember words swallowed, bitten back. And will, like him, solitary rooster, insatiable optimist, insurgent

soul, awaken, scratch for seed and boldly sing the sun up once again.

LA ANIMA

—La Calle Anima, Havana, Cuba

The woman in green taffeta sauntering the street, *la Anima*. Her broad
shoulders and hipless torso is the body of a man *en la calle Anima*.

La Anima, streets of stickball, children's crack of a bat to bottle cap, vapors
rising from the week old trash, the sweet rot of garbage, *la Anima*.

La Anima, the men bent over chessboards, the sweat on their glasses of beer,
La Anima, the crumbling buildings

standing in quiet dignity, *la Anima*, the tree sprouting from an abandoned
building's roof, *la Anima*, the hope. The woman in white

robes and a mouth puckered with time, *la Anima*. *La Anima*, the distant
drumming coming from the apartment

across the street, the drums of ancestors rising. *La Anima*, the woman with
meaty arms, full breasts swelling

in her brassiere, Afro hair, who leans over the balcony calling to a man's
slight retreating frame below,

"Faggot! Lazy faggot! You do nothing around here." *La Anima*.
The streets are silent.

The men look up from their rum. The children stop swinging their stick.
The two gringos on the balcony look up

from their books. *La Anima.* Finally a pudgy man in chains says something back in Spanish. The street erupts in laughter, *la Anima.*

The tourists sit and watch—the man with gray eyes, gray hair, and the woman dark as one of them. *La Anima.*

A maroon-haired woman lowers bootlegged liquor down a rope, *la Anima.* The people gather in the street, *la Anima.* The gringo tourists still watch.

The woman turns to the man as if to say, "On a long hot day a cold gray man must do," when what she wants is to burst

into the streets. But when the streets will not allow you to speak of the dictator (whose name people don't dare say

without a lilt to their voice) or of the country, hers, that has cut them off like a rotted limb—still she wants

their buoyant joy, *la Anima,* and the heavy truth, *la Anima,* which tethers them all to the street.

THE ABSOLUTE VALUE OF LONELINESS

It's hard to quantify certain things. In Havana, though I know how much my government doesn't want me here, I walk deeper into the sun-

stunned streets, the blue, green and pink buildings, deeper into the sweet-stink of alley garbage, past the men drinking rum, hunched

over dominoes, the kids swinging a stick to hit a plastic bottle cap. In America, there is no place to go when the loneliness gets too thick

to walk through, except a bar, which breeds more lonely. Until the bar, full of shadows catching shadows,

glows with something akin to love while the dark hides the shame of being human. But now, a woman

and a man with skin like a toasted almond break through my thought-barrier. "Come with us."

Their broken English cobbles together a bridge. My feet decide to step forward and walk it

with them, their laughter lighting up the street like firefly-constellations. I'm not sure where we're going, but it doesn't matter.

In their house are cousins with hats turned backwards, smelling of soapy cologne; uncles with winking gold teeth and kind eyes who,

rum-weary, nod off in wicker chairs, while small children scatter like mice under the roofless house. Rumba throbs

through the speakers. How can anyone feel lonely in a world like this, even I, who feel alone everywhere?

A woman with a bright white grin and eyes that refuse to look away teaches
me to salsa. Moving my hips in figure

eights, I remember the idea of an absolute value. How a negative attaches
itself to a number, the way many times

in this life, loneliness has to me. Joliet was too landlocked, too small to fit
my mother's shadow, I lost

too many friends to fishtailing in the cornfields, to suburbs, to the
Republican Party. New York was too filled with light

and the star of my desire always a hair's breadth away. Cape Cod was too
small, and the whales couldn't save me.

But today I am moving in the sign of infinity, passing a bottle of rum with
these people I will never see again,

and for once I don't feel alone. For once, it is okay to be lost amid people
who don't dare speak a word about their dictator.

People who face famine when a hurricane blows over their delicate chickens.
People who are still dancing past a history

of slaves bent like black scythes over the cane fields, who are dancing into
the present second, who still will be dancing long after I leave.

When I go home to a street that won't allow me to dance, they'll be with
me and I with them. My hand and foot extended.

Not knowing how to take the next step, but infinitely moved.

ACKNOWLEDGMENTS

Poems in this book have been published in slightly different forms in the following publications:

THE DEAD MULE SCHOOL OF SOUTHERN LITERATURE:
"Infinite Things" and "A Night Back in Joliet, Illinois."
MAIN STREET RAG: "Mink Rooftop."
DOUBLE LIVES, REINVENTION, AND THOSE WE LEAVE
BEHIND ANTHOLOGY: "Love Poem to a Tree," and "The First Person."
THE NEW YORK QUARTERLY: "Smashing Toilets." "Hymn to the
Midwest That Meanders," and "American Romance" are forthcoming.
THE NEW PLAINS REVIEW: "Smashing Toilets" is reprinted.
THE SYCAMORE REVIEW: "Painting of a Truck."
TAR RIVER POETRY: "The Yellow Jeep."
HARPUR PALATE: "Advice to Dan's Next Girlfriend, From the Ghosts of
Lovers Past."
POET LORE: "The Absolute Value of Loneliness."
THE CHICAGO QUARTERLY REVIEW: "Watching Bergman Films
With My Mother."
BOXCAR POETRY REVIEW: "Wild, Wild Horses."
THE SARANAC REVIEW: "*La Anima*" and "The Buddhist Experiences a
Moment of Reluctance."
INKWELL: "Cockfight" and "My Version of Freedom."
WAIT A MINUTE, I HAVE I TAKE OFF MY BRA ANTHOLOGY: "My
Mother's Nipples."

Thanks to Vermont Studio Center, The Santa Fe Art Institute, The Squaw
Valley Community of Writers, The Breadloaf Writers' Conference, the Palm
Beach Poetry Festival, and The Authors' League Fund for their generous
grants and fellowships that have helped in the writing of this book.

I would also like to thank Heather Tosteson for the immeasurable time,
mentorship, and wisdom she devoted to preparing this manuscript and
Charles Brockett for giving the same gift. Jeannette Angell, Fred Biddle,

Kaveh Bassiri, Paul Cezanne, and Bruce Van Allen. Sharon Charde for granting me the permission to use her lines, "With you he may need some Cialis" and "He'll never love you as much as he loves me," and all members of the Wising Up Press Editorial Collective, especially Kathleen Housley and Natalie Tilghman.

Maria Nazos was raised in Athens, Greece and Joliet, Illinois. She earned her MFA in Creative Writing from Sarah Lawrence College. She has received writing grants and fellowships from Vermont Studio Center, The Santa Fe Art Institute, The Squaw Valley Community of Writers, and the Palm Beach Poetry Festival. Her poetry has appeared in numerous literary journals such as *The New York Quarterly, The Sycamore Review*, and *Poet Lore*, and was selected as runner up for the Philbrick Athenaeum Poetry Project Award. She lives and writes in Provincetown, Massachusetts.

CPSIA information can be obtained at www.ICGtesting.com
Printed in the USA
BVOW05s1146170216

437066BV00001B/22/P